color

and the

EDGAR CAYCE

READINGS

by

Roger Lewis

ARE PRESS

ASSOCIATION FOR
RESEARCH AND
ENLIGHTENMENT

A.R.E. PRESS   •   VIRGINIA BEACH   •   VIRGINIA

ISBN 87604-068-7

24th Printing, February 2003

A.R.E. Press
215 67th Street
Virginia Beach, VA 23451-2061

ACKNOWLEDGEMENT
The A.R.E. Press gratefully acknowledges the courtesy of the following copyright holder for permission to use excerpts:

From COLOR IN YOUR WORLD by Faber Birren (© The Crowell-Collier Publishing Company 1962)

Cover design by Richard A. Horwege

Printed in the U.S.A.

CONTENTS

INTRODUCTION

Throughout the ages color has been replete with symbolism, and vestiges of the ancient lore appear in the rituals of the Church, in mythology, and in the phrases of our everyday speech. In *Color and the Edgar Cayce Readings,* the author, Roger Lewis, an artist, has uniquely combined rather divergent approaches to color symbolism. First, he sets the stage with the scientific examination of color. Then, using Edgar Cayce's booklet *Auras,* he shows how the conscious Cayce interpreted various colors when they appeared in the emanation of light around an individual. Because the Cayce readings associated various colors with the seven spiritual centers in the body, Mr. Lewis traces the colors on the path of the kundalini, describing the influences of the endocrine glands. Finally, the author looks at his subject from the point of view of the color psychologist, and indicates what the color specialist Faber Birren had to say about color preferences and personality traits. This introductory study might well be said to be viewing color physically, mentally and spiritually in a harmonious blend.   *Violet M. Shelley*
                Editor

Chapter One

WHAT IS COLOR?

Many theories have been expounded on the subject of how to use color for healing, for personality identification, and for effective color harmony in wearing apparel and in our environment. Medical science tends to discount the possibility of any value in color as a healing agent. Psychologists and psychiatrists, on the other hand, have made extensive use of color in the analysis of mental illness. However, their findings, based on the continued observation of patients, deal basically with the negative or destructive personality traits and emotions.

We cannot live without color. This essence of the life force is all about us. It can make chills run up and down the spine or quicken the soul. If we step into an air-conditioned room which has been painted gray we will undoubtedly complain because it is too cold; yet if the color is orange we will feel most comfortable. Psychologists say that tasks which require muscular effort will be best performed in an environment of warm colors which stimulate and speed up the pulse. If a task involves mental concentration, the calm atmosphere of tranquil blues and greens will serve best.

We can separate the color spectrum into two basic groups: the exciting, vibrant red-orange-yellow group; and the passive, calm blue-green group. Individuals who favor the first group are more likely to be extroverts — easily influenced, impressionable and social. There is a great possibility that those who favor the second group will have an attitude of detachment, showing greater interest in themselves than in the world about them. Naturally quiet, they will probably be deliberate and introspective.

Blue is preferred more often by introverts and conservative people, red by extroverts. Yellow is the choice of the intellectual, while well-balanced individuals choose green. Faber Birren, in his book, *Color in Your World,* suggests that there may be a third personality type, "ambiverts." Artistic persons usually thrive on purple.

We react to color at an unconscious level and acknowledge color symbolism in the idioms of our language. Some people paint the town red, become entangled in red tape, must read only red-hot news and may turn purple with rage if they can't find a red cent in their pockets. A novice may be green even though he is a blue-blood and once in a blue moon he may feel blue. Through it all he may even be true-blue.

A policeman in anything but blue wouldn't seem the same. Red is universally accepted as a danger or stop sign while yellow means caution or quarantine. We mourn in black, identify red and green with Christmas, green with medicine and purple with law. Color is undoubtedly one of the most dominating influences in our day-to-day existence and yet it is an influence we take very much for granted.

Scientists tell us that we receive all knowledge of the universe through electromagnetic radiation. What we see with the eye alone — visible light — comprises only a very narrow band of that electromagnetic spectrum. There is a dual property to the nature of light: it acts in a pattern of long and short waves and in a particulate or corpuscular form.

Generally, there is a very close relationship between electromagnetic radiation and the atomic structure of matter. The atom is made up of a series of electrons revolving about a central nucleus. Now and then one of these orbiting electrons is released, or there is a radical alteration of the nucleus itself, thereby creating waves of energy. The direction of this electromagnetic radiation, or light, which fills the vacuum of space, is affected by powerful gravitational fields. It is also capable of being bent or refracted.

When visible light — that almost infinitesimal segment of energy waves out of the total spectrum of electromagnetic radiation — is passed through a prism, or is refracted (bent) or is reflected from a grating which has been marked with a series of fine lines, it is spread into rainbow-like colors — a spectrum sequence ranging from short wavelengths to long wavelengths: violet, indigo, blue, green, yellow, orange and red.

This field of energy is all about us. What we perceive as a result of this energy is illusion — only the energy itself is real. Color does not exist in actuality. It is only a sensation in our consciousness. In other words, what we see with our eyes is not the object itself but is a series of various wavelengths of light, traveling at the same rate of speed, being reflected from the object. The object itself is colorless. Some wavelengths are absorbed by the object while others are reflected. The atomic and molecular structure of a yellow object, for instance, is such that it absorbs all wavelengths except yellow, which is reflected to the eye. We are affected by these wavelengths of light, or color, as the vibration is passed on to the brain or to that portion of the cerebral cortex at the back of the head that is known as the striate area.

The only colors recognized as "real" for three centuries have been those that Sir Isaac Newton saw and reported in 1672 when he passed a narrow stream of sunlight through a prism. Since then each of the seven spectral colors he saw, from violet to red, have been assigned to a definite segment of the spectrum, whose wavelength is commonly measured in millimicrons.

Newton identified and called what he saw the seven "homogeneal" colors: violet, indigo, blue, green, yellow, orange and red. The cornerstone of all color theory today has remained essentially the same as his proposition that "Light consists of rays differently refrangible. To the same degree of refrangibility ever belongs the same degree of refrangibility."

More simply, then, every red-colored light, when passed through a prism, will be bent to the same degree characterizing all red light, having a definite range of wavelengths. Each color, consequently, has its own wavelength, with violet having the shortest visible wavelength and each color in order being longer, down to red, which has the longest visible wavelength.

Newton went on to show that objects appear to be colored because they absorb certain wavelengths and reflect others, and that it is the reflected rays that reach the eye, indicating shape, form and color. He demonstrated further that there is a complementary color for each color and that the approximation of white light could be achieved through the combination of any two complementary colors. Newton, himself, was unable to produce a pure white, but others who continued to experiment with his theories were able to do so.

By mixing the light from any two colors in his spectrum, Newton was able to produce a color which was intermediate, i.e., yellow, by mixing red and green light; cyan (blue-green) from blue and green light; and purple (a color not thought to be in the spectrum at all) by mixing red and blue light. The primary colors used in this experiment are referred to as *additive* primaries: red, blue and green. On the other hand, the mixing of pigments which produce the reflected

3

light of *subtractive* primary colors — red, blue and yellow — creates purple from red and blue, green from blue and yellow, and orange from yellow and red.

We note, in reference to Newton's producing a yellow by mixing red and green, that this has to do with mixing red and green "light" rather than pigment. The sensation of yellowness is somewhat of a phenomenon and is thought to be due to a simultaneous stimulation of both the red- and green-sensitive cones in the retina. This is based upon the three-color theory of vision, a theory developed by others from Newton's reverse prismatic experiments attempting to produce white by combining the light of all seven colors of the spectrum, and then by combining the lights of complementary colors. When light touches the eye, each separate cone reacts in accordance with its sensitivity as well as the make-up of the light-waves, and there is complete color sensation produced in the brain as a result of the three responses. This is illustrated in the production of a yellow sensation through the mixture of pure red light (containing no true yellow light) with pure green light (likewise containing no yellow light). This theory assumes that the eye contains no actual yellow-sensitive cones. This is similar to what happens when one stares at a spot of red for a moment or two. When the red spot is removed, a green spot seems to take its place.

The conditions under which we see color is the first question that must be dealt with in any theory of color. Newton's explanation, embellished through continued theorizing by others, is the basis of our understanding of color today, but Newton, the physicist, had very little concern for the physiological activities of the organs involved in the sensation of color — the eye and the brain.

Thomas Young, the English physicist and physician, came up with a hypothesis in 1801 that there are three types of receptors, or nerve endings, in the eye and that each is sensitive to one of the three primary colors: red, green and blue. His idea was lost for fifty years, however, until the great German scientist, Helmholtz, picked it up and made it an integral part of classical color theory even though it was unproved. Another brilliant physicist in the mid 1800s, J. Clerk Maxwell, developed and demonstrated a mathematical formula for mixing the primary colors to produce any desired hue. He also produced the world's first color photograph in 1855 by combining individual black and white plates which had been exposed through red, green and blue filters. His original demonstration led to the development of modern color photography techniques and to color television.

4

It was further suggested that there must be some sort of "fatigue" mechanism, within the eye or its nerve connections to the brain, which reverses itself in order to effect a complementary afterimage. An easy way to see this color in an objective sense is to concentrate on a brightly colored spot for about three minutes. The afterimage of the spot will *appear* as its complementary color when the spot is removed. For example, if the spot is red, the afterimage will be blue-green. Although this concept was acceptable, color experiences that could not be made to fit into the Newtonian concept were considered to be psychological distortions or untrue.

Edwin Land, of Polaroid-Land Corporation, challenged classical color theory at its very foundations around 1955. He took up Maxwell's three-color system and was immensely astonished to find that there was no need of the blue record of the original scene. He discovered that he could project the shorter wavelength, green, without a filter and yet come up with a most satisfactory color picture. After his successful demonstration, Land learned that his system had been discovered as early as 1914. Evidently disbelief had caused the method to be ignored and forgotten, for classical color had no provision for such a phenomenon.

Since Newton, many theories as to how vision and color operate have been expounded. None of them is conclusive. Dr. Max Luscher, the eminent Swiss psychologist, differs somewhat from the Cayce readings when he discounts instinctive and reactive response to color and attributes it entirely to development and education. Birren writes that "color preferences are innate in most individuals. In other words, you were born with a liking for particular colors, and what you feel about them will probably last throughout your life."

Man is not only surrounded with color but also has a love for it. He expresses his emotions through color and has made it an almost commonplace aspect of his life. Whether he realizes it or not, contemporary man has assimilated, with historical consistency, the character and whim of color as it relates to both divine and human meaning, mysticism, the riddles of life and death and the puzzling ways of creation.

There is little, if any, doubt that all living things are affected by visible light and color in one way or another. We all know from simple observation that visible light is necessary for the growth of plant life, and numerous experiments indicate that growth is restrained by ultraviolet and infrared wavelengths. Most medical scientists on the other hand, may not admit that wavelengths or vibrations visible to the human eye have any useful purpose to the human organism other than sight, although it does make use of infrared and ultraviolet radiation in the treatment of certain physiological conditions.

The Edgar Cayce readings, in addition to confirming scientific theories insofar as they have gone, pick up where the scientists have left off and tell us what happens to color vibrations within the physical body, whether these vibrations are received from an external source or are generated by the cells within.

Later chapters discuss the individual colors in relationship to each of the seven endocrine glands and suggest that with each of the seven colors, as with every action we take, we have a choice: we can use each color vibration constructively or we can use it destructively. We can use it in harmony with the Creative Forces or we can use it for selfish or self-satisfying purposes.

As has been indicated, these are channels, these are opportunities. For what purpose? For fame or fortune alone? or that ye may be a helpful influence? If the motives are selfish, little success. If they are for the universal forces or sources, that God may be the greater glory in the lives of others through thine own feeble effort, then success. For know, ye alone with the Lord are a *great* majority! 1494-1

Chapter Two

VIBRATION – MOVEMENT – COLOR

The Cayce readings tell us very simply that color is *vibration* or *movement* and that it is both a positive and a negative force. There is no attempt to explain it in technical terms or to go into the complicated details of the number of wavelengths for each color. Those are considerations for the more scientific mind. Instead, the readings advise us to know ourselves first if we would know the universe.

> . . . for each cell in the atomic force of the body is as a world of its own, and each one – each cell – being in perfect unison, may build to that [which is] necessary to reconstruct the forces of the body in all its needs . . .   93-1

There is the implication that only when each cell, each atom, of the physical body vibrates in perfect harmony can constructive forces supply the needs of the body. The following reading asks specifically if the activity within self is positive in its relationship to color.

> . . . consider the effect of the color itself upon thine own body as ye attempt to apply same by either concentration, dedication or meditating upon these. For as has been given, color is but vibration. Vibration is movement. Movement is activity of a positive or negative force. Is the activity of self as in relationship to these then positive?   281-29

The booklet *Auras* quotes Edgar Cayce as saying that color "seems to be a characteristic of the vibration of matter, and our souls seem to reflect it in this three-dimensional world through atomic patterns. We are patterns, and we project colors which are there for those who can see them."

Does this mean that because man was created in the image of God, the Creative Force, man reflects color – this characteristic of God – through atomic activity within? This statement and various

7

readings indicate that the source of life itself is the same as color (light), and that both creative vibration, which is indispensable to the regenerative forces in our material plane, and destructive vibration are from the same source. The difference comes about in the way we use that energy.

> Life in its manifestation is vibration. Electricity is vibration. But vibration that is creative is one thing. Vibration that is destructive is another. Yet they may be from the same source. 1861-16

Scientists come close to admitting that *vibration* and God are the same when they tell us that all knowledge of the Universe is received through electromagnetic radiation. The readings state in definite terms that *creative vibration is* God.

> Electricity or vibration is that same energy, same power, ye call God. Not that God is an electric light or an electric machine, but that vibration that is creative is of that same energy as life itself. 2828-4

Not only is every physical body a receptor of color — this electromagnetic radiation — but the body itself is continually radiating the same energy both within and without. For, just as this energy is created by the release of electrons from the atom in space, the same radiation is created by the release of electrons from the atoms that make up the physical body. Are we in harmony with the Creative Force? Are we in harmony within ourselves? Are we building constructively or are we using this force destructively?

> . . . the body is built up by the radiation of vibratory forces from each and every unit of the body functioning in its proper manner. 283-1

What is the *proper manner* that builds up rather than destroys?

> . . . man — by his compliance with Divine Law — [brings] order out of chaos; or, by his disregard of the associations and laws of Divine influence, [brings] chaos and *destructive* forces into his experience. 416-7

Then, whether it is order under Divine Law or disregard of Divine Law, the physical body will radiate those vibrations that identify one's own inner being. We will reflect our own ideals.

> All bodies radiate those vibrations with which it, the body, controls itself in mental, in physical, and such radiation is called the aura. 5756-1

Color and sound are "just different rates of vibration," according to reading 2779-1. Misapplication of vibrations, color or sound can bring about the destruction of self.

> Man may *mis*apply [his] own creative force, then become a destruction to self. Man's applying that force in that channel in which that is directed gives light, life and abundance, in every way and manner. 900-227

We are further enjoined to learn the basic forces or basic principles of color as they relate to the bodily forces so that we will have another effective tool to help us in our task of building creatively.

Then later they become the activities or the associations . . . For as has been indicated . . . this necessarily becomes a basic force or principle for the very activity. But it would also be well to learn the activity of the etheronic and the vibrations of the body, for these are they that produce color, that produce aura, that produce the activities seen *as* color.   1436-3

Scientists do not tell us what happens to these various colors, or wavelengths, other than to tell us that this is the way sight or vision functions, although they are beginning to delve into this aspect much more. The Cayce readings, however, state that these vibrations are disseminated throughout the physical body and have an effect upon the growth of the physical body, the mental body and the spiritual body.

. . . tones and sounds will be the channel through which the coordinating of forces for the body may make for the first of the perfect reactions . . .   758-38

The vibrations we create within ourselves, from our own atomic structure, the vibrations we reflect of those received from without, mirror our own souls through the colors about us and our color preferences. If we are to have physical, mental and spiritual growth, we must use these vibrations harmoniously in a constructive and creative manner.

In the harmony of sound, the harmony of color, even the harmony of motion itself, its beauty is all akin to that expression of the soul-self in the harmony of the mind, if used properly in relationship to [the] body.   3659-1

In other words, all vibrations, color, sound and motion, this vast energy that is all about us, are of the God-Force itself, and are here to aid us in our growth and progress toward the *oneness* which is our ultimate purpose.

. . . all vibration, color, and color with radiation . . . is to set the vibrations in the body for body-forces . . .   3370-1

As these body-forces are activated, similar vibrations are activated in mind and soul and the energies radiate about the body itself. These radiations, these colors, or *aura,* which emanate from the physical body reflect the physical and mental condition of the body.

All bodies radiate those vibrations with which it, the body, controls itself in mental, in physical, and such radiation is called the aura. The mediums, or a psychic in certain phases of psychic phenomena, gain their impressions from such radiation.   5756-1

9

In the chapter on meditation in *A Search for God,* we are told: "Vibrations which are emanations of life from within are material expressions of a spiritual influence, a force that emanates from life itself." And reading 3491-1 directs us to "Find that light in self. It isn't the light of the noonday sun, nor the moon, but rather of the Son of man." When that light has been found and activated, the soul, infinitesimal though it may be, can express itself in any way in any part of the universe.

With the awareness of the soul and its role as an everlasting vital force or activity comes an awareness of the vibratory activity that travels through the nervous system of the body.

> Ye are told that such an awareness is an activity of consciousness that passes along the nervous system to and from the brain. Then, just the same there are contacts with that which is eternal within thy physical body. For there is the bowl that must one day be broken . . .   281-41

> . . . to know, to understand, that there is a *definite* connection between that we have chosen to term the sixth sense, or acting through the auditory forces of the body-physical, and the other self within self.   5754-1

Within the physical body, we are told, there are seven glandular centers: the pituitary, the pineal, the thyroid, the thymus, the adrenals (or solar plexus), the Leydig and the gonads. Scientists generally admit a lack of understanding of the function of these endocrine, or ductless, glands in their relationship to color. The Cayce readings, on the other hand, explain this relationship in some detail in the *Revelation* readings.

> *Q-1. Do the colors vary for each center with different individuals, or may definite colors be associated with each center?*

> A-1. Both. For to each — remember, to study each of these in the light not only of what has just been given, but that as is a practical experience in the material world — as is known, vibration is the essence or the basis of color. As color and vibration then become to the consciousness along the various centers in an individual's experience in meditation made aware, they come to mean definite experiences. Just as anger is red, or as something depressing is blue, yet in their shades, their tones, their activities, to each they begin with the use of same in the experience to mean those various stages. For instance, while red is anger, rosy to most souls means delight and joy — yet to others, as they are formed in their transmission from center to center, come to mean or to express what *manner* of joy; whether that as would arise from a material, a mental, or a spiritual experience. Just as may be seen in the common interpretation of white, but with all manner of rays from same begins or comes to mean that [which is] above the aura of all in its vibration from the body and from the activity of the mental experience when the various centers are vibrating to color.   281-30

Chapter Three

SOURCE OF COLOR PREFERENCE

Throughout the readings there are references to past lives in the earth as well as planetary sojourns between lives, as represented by astrological aspects. Attitudinal and emotional vibrations, both positive and negative, acquired by the soul either in a previous life or during interims between incarnations, are carried over by the soul into its present physical existence. These vibrations may manifest as the color preferences of the individual and may reflect the conditions he has brought with him.

> Thus we find that the sojourns about the earth, during the interims between earthly sojourns, are called the astrological aspects. Not that an entity may have manifested physically on such planets; but [rather] in that consciousness which is the consciousness of that environ. And these [consciousnesses] have been accredited with certain potential influences in the mental aspect of an entity.   2144-1

These urges may be indications of progression or regression in the journey toward oneness.

> That absent from the material body is manifested in what we call astrological aspects, that become a phase of each and every soul — and are as signposts along the individual way . . . these are a part of thy heritage, thy innate urge; that arise from, and produces influences in, the material experiences in the present.   1745-1

Psychologists who believe that color preferences reflect the individual's personality have devised many tests, such as the Luscher Color Test, to chart attitudes and emotions, particularly those hidden deep within the person. The readings indicate that they mirror his individuality as well as his personality.

11

> The shadows of those things from the sojourns of this entity in Mercury, Jupiter, Saturn, Uranus, Venus and the influences of the general system's activity as in the Sun and Moon, have their portion [influence] in the very relationships and activity of the entity. These [astrological influences] are but the mental urges that arise, and become as the *individuality* of an entity in expression in the material world; while the appearances in the earth through the various sojourns that [have] become active in the experience of an entity at any one given place or position or appearance or period are as but the personality in the entity's experience – and are as the urges from the emotions that have been created.   633-2

An example of this is seen in a reading given for [1406] in which a determination to express an overabundance of self-esteem, a negative aspect acquired from Mercury (indigo), is in direct conflict with a creative aspect acquired from a sojourn in Saturn (red), thereby manifesting in the entity's present physical condition.

This excessive feeling of self-esteem, or self-importance, at the area of the pineal gland, or Christ-Consciousness center, is reflected as a rejection of the color *indigo,* resulting in a suppression of sensitivity. Such an individual delights in "putting on a show" of his tastefulness and graciousness. At the same time, he is very critical of others, refusing to accept anything or anyone as genuine.

An attitude such as this causes the individual to direct his creative activity toward the fulfillment of his own successes or conquests and a desire to experience every physical aspect of earthly existence. This is indicated by a preference for red, the color of the gonad center.

The conflict created between the rejected indigo and the preferred red can lead to outbursts of suppressed agitation from trying to resist the positive influences of the pineal center. Its results may be irritability, anger, frustration or even sexual obsessions, possibly leading to heart trouble or ulcers.

> In the astrological aspects we find the entity headstrong from Mercury, yet very demure in its headstrongness, and oft sets itself to have its way – eventually has it and finds it isn't what was wanted at all. These [conditions] arise from the conflicting influences from Mercury, with Saturn.
> Hence many changes in the aspects . . .   1406-1

> For it is not strange that music, color, vibration are all a part of the planets, just as the planets are a part – and a pattern – of the whole universe.   5755-1

This pattern is part of the Universal Law. Each planetary, or color, influence is there for the benefit of each individual soul. It is up to each soul to choose the direction of his activity in relation to that influence.

12

> Begin with the spiritual attitude. Find that, and ye will begin then with the correct attitude. For, that we find in spirit taketh form in mind. Mind becomes the builder. The physical body is the result. 3359-1

If we are to find our way back to the Creator, then, we must strive for that at-onement with the Creative Forces, and this is dependent upon our willingness to make our purposes and desires harmonize with the purposes and desires of the Universal Forces.

We have brought color preferences and vibrations with us from prior sojourns, and it is what we do with them that makes the difference as to whether we become a constructive or a destructive force in the material plane. If we use these urges, these colors, these vibrations creatively through each incarnation, through each planetary sojourn — for it is through this pattern of incarnation that we evolve — we will find our way back to the Oneness.

> For, without passing through each and every stage of development, there is not the correct vibration to become one with the Creator . . .
>
> Then, in the many stages of development, throughout the universal or in the great system of the universal forces . . . each stage of development [is] made manifest through flesh, which is the testing portion of the universal vibration. In this manner then, and for this reason, all [are] made manifest in flesh, and [there is the] development through the eons of time, space, and *called* eternity. 900-16

Chapter Four

VIOLET

The shortest wavelength of electromagnetic radiation (light), to which we have given the name *violet,* is associated with the *pituitary gland* by the Cayce readings. It is further identified with the church *Laodicia* in the Revelation, with the planet *Jupiter,* and with *Father* in the Lord's Prayer.

Science has determined that vision in the human body is dependent upon the interaction of the retinal nucleus, the mid-brain, the pituitary gland and the inter-connecting network of nerve fibers. German scientist Richard Becker said, in 1953, that the function of this nerve network is to distinguish and to identify color and to determine the esthetic reaction to it. Beyond this the scientific world seems to be at a loss to explain how this nerve network and glandular system functions in respect to vibrations or color, or even if there is an individual color relationship with each of the glands. Dr. Max Luscher suggested that there is a lack of understanding of the pituitary function and indicated that much more research is needed in this direction. The Cayce readings agree with him in this respect.

> For, as given, few have conceived of – or attempted to analyze – the effect created in a physical body through the *mental* impressions received, or conceded that there is an activity spiritually that may go on in active force within the human body.   281-51

This energy, or electromagnetic vibration, is all about us, then, and whether it is received through the eye, the cells of the body, or spiritually, it is the essence of the Creative Force and does have a definite effect upon the physical body.

> Is the First Cause, then, that the separation of God in the desire for companionship with Himself, that as created or brought into a material

14

> manifestation the reverse of love, of hope, of patience, of all the attributes that are the spirit of activity, the moving influence or force?
>
> This we see manifested in a physical body through the glandular system — as the activity of conception, the dividing of the activity of the gland itself, that brings conception. 281-51

These color vibrations are disseminated, then, to each of the seven endocrine glands, each absorbing one particular wavelength and passing the remaining on to the other glands in turn.

> It has been given at first that as each organ develops in the foetus there is the development of the gland within itself to give it the ability to *reproduce* itself. Yet there are those outside, or they are centers from and through which pass the emotions, the activities from the organs of other portions of the body; and become so influenced as to produce a definite *physical* effect.
>
> If they produce the definite mental effect, if they produce through same definite spiritual attributes or abilities, and if these are coordinated by the individual into personality — what are the results?
>
> Here this is illustrated in Samson — a lad who grew to manhood with the unusual strength and power, the ability to cope with exterior forces and influences that were beyond the understanding and comprehension of his associates. Yet his ability to say no to the opposite sex was nil — his ability not to be influenced by the opposite sex was nil — because of the desire for the gratification of those activities which were of a glandular nature within the body. 281-49

As the readings reiterate, *mind is the builder.* If the mental body is in perfect harmony with the Creative Forces, the colors will reach each center in pure form. If the thoughts within the mental body are negative in nature, the colors passing to the centers will be out of balance to the same degree as the mental activity.

> Thus, this is the first of the centers from which arises all that is movement, to bring into being both the face and the preface — or the back, or the reverse — in the experience. It carries with it, what? That *mind!* For, remember, ever, the pattern is ever the same — Mind the builder! 281-51

The same reading tells us that once the light vibrations have been received by the mind, the first movement is to the *pituitary* gland "which either fades or becomes a channel along which there may move the power and might to find expression through the very activities of the organs of the body itself."

What is the pituitary gland? What is its function? According to various scientific sources, it is an endocrine gland (hypophysis) about one centimeter in diameter, which secretes substances that constrict the blood vessels and raises the arterial blood pressure. This *maestro* of the endocrine palette exerts a controlling influence over the other endocrine glands. The two lobes of the pituitary are located behind the orbits and just below the base of the brain. They are surrounded by the *half shell* of the *sella turcia* of the sphenoid bone.

Most dictionaries describe the pituitary as a small, oval endocrine, or ductless gland which lies close to the center of the brain in a depression of the sphenoid bone, supplying the blood stream with several important hormones. The readings tell us that the pituitary

> . . . is the way along the system. (This is going backward — we should begin with the first cause, if an understanding is to be maintained!) These, they pass along the way; that has to do with the correlating of physical, mental and spiritual understanding. It is the growth of body and mind, the opening of which is the arousing in the adolescent to the disputations that become the conflicting influences in the experience of the individual entity.
>
> It is the door, as interpreted by some, through which physically all of the reflex actions respond through the various forces of the nerve system.
>
> It is that to and through which the mental activities come that produce the influences in the imaginative system as well as the racial prejudices as termed the predominating influences — or the blood force itself.
>
> In the spiritual, it is that to which the singleness in the adult brings the awakening to its capabilities, its possibilities, its ultimate hope and desire.
>
> It is that which in the change period brings the physical influence in which there is the correlating by experience, through the changing influences in body as related to its *own* findings and its individual intent and purpose. Or, as may be termed, it is physically the ripening of the fruit of the experience of the body; as to whether it has been material-mindedness or of spiritual import.
>
> In the mental it is that which gives judgment and understanding, tolerance *and* relationships to the determining factors. Hence we find some grow old gracefully, some tolerantly, some fussily and some very meanly. All of these, then, are the expressions of that which has been the dominant force that began from its first active influence that passed from its innate to the animate, to its full completion in the individual experience of the entity.
>
> This is the influence also, or the activities spoken of, as the door upon and through which the old men may dream dreams, the young men may see visions.   281-58

Violet, the color of royalty, is associated with the pituitary center, which is called by the medical profession the *master gland* of the endocrine system. When this gland is opened through proper attunement to its Creative Source, however, its color becomes *golden,* the color of the new man, the symbol of the Father, or of Heaven.

16

The pituitary gland is the controlling center. According to the readings, the pituitary is ruled by Jupiter. The Jupiterean influence is dualistic in its endowment of benevolent urges and adverse desires.

From the Jupiterean sojourn we find not only the benevolent but the adverse forces. 1990-3

In Jupiter we find the great ennobling influences, the broad-mindedness, the ability to consider others, the universal consciousnesses that are a part of the entity's unfoldment. 2890-2

Astrologists indicate that the positive influence of Jupiter will endow the individual with fortunate circumstances in all areas of his life. Money is gained easily and the individual will make wise use of it.

In Jupiter's forces we find . . . those conditions that would bring the monies and the forces of good in the life. 900-14

If the individual choosing violet as a favorite color makes positive choices, he will have a well-rounded personality, good mental abilities with fine reasoning faculties, strength of character and good judgment. There will be a high sense of personal integrity and attraction to others. Negative choices would indicate self-centeredness, and an overbearing nature.

Birren says: "If you favor purple you automatically assume — by right or by desire — an uncommon quality among the mortals of this earth. Perhaps you deserve the association. If you do, you have a good mind, a rare wit, and an ability to observe things which go unnoticed by others. You may be both introspective and temperamental — a combination that epitomizes the artist. You are sensitive; you relish the subtle and can see magnificence in both the baroque and the humble."

There is indecision, inconsistency and aloofness in the individual who prefers violet, according to Birren. Although he is naturally creative, often a genius, he may be vain and revel in the admiration of others.

According to the Luscher Color Test, an individual preferring violet enjoys the refinements of living, is tactful and warm, while retaining an attitude of censure. He must be certain of another's integrity and genuineness before he will accept him. Such a person keeps his emotions under rigid and vigilant control and covers his own overly trusting nature by demanding complete honesty from others.

When the pituitary gland, the master-gland of the physical body, is opened through meditation, the vibration of violet is lifted, or changed, to golden. This is brought about through the complete acceptance of the ways of the Creative Force. As we live the precept of "Not my will, but Thine," we experience a joyful and peaceful kind of living that can only be understood through the experiencing of it. As our faults and inadequacies are overcome, the violet vibration becomes so pure in golden richness that it is perceived as white, or the unity of all colors, and all of the seven spiritual centers return to their original purposes, recharged and regenerated.

> Then as each entity under a given name makes its correlating of that it does about the Creative Forces in its experience, it is coming under those influences that are being fed by the manna — which is a representation of the universality as well as the stability of purposes in the Creative Forces as manifested to a group or a nation of peoples.
> So it becomes that as the Master gave, "Ye shall not live by bread alone but by every word that proceedeth from the mouth of the Father."
> That indeed is the holy manna which each entity, each soul in each experience must make a part of its mental and spiritual self. Thus it becomes as is indicated, in that the name — as in each experience — bears a relative relationship to the development of the individual entity in each experience.
> Then in the end, or in those periods indicated, it is when each entity, each soul has so manifested, so acted in its relationships as to become then as the new name; white, clear, known only to him that hath overcome. Overcome what? The world, even as He.   281-31

It is at this point that we come into the harmony of complete at-onement with the Creative Force, where all of our vibrations, colors, sounds, and relationships with others come together in unity of purpose.

> All of these have not only the attunement of a vibration but of color, harmony; and all those relative relationships as one to another.
> Then as has been asked, and has been indicated in another portion of Revelation, all those that bear the mark, those that have the name, those that have the stone — these are representatives then of the same experience in the various phases of an individual experience for its activity.
> Then the interpretation is that they *have* overcome, they *have* the new name, they *have* the manna, they *have* the understanding, they *have* their relationships as secure in the blood of the Lamb!   281-31

The following questions and answers from the readings on the Revelation are particularly important in understanding the pituitary gland, and thus the colors violet, gold and white:

> *Q-3. Which is the highest gland in the body — the pineal or the pituitary?*
> A-3. The pituitary!

Q-4. Are we correct in interpreting the 24 elders as the 24 cranial nerves of the head especially related to the 5 senses?

A-4. Correct.

Q-5. Is the frequent reference to the throne indicating the head in which are found the higher gland centers?

A-5. Correct.

Q-31. What is meant by the 7 lamps of fire burning before the throne, described as the 7 spirits of God — Ch. 4:5?

A-31. Those influences or forces which in their activity in the natures of man are without, that stand ever before the throne of grace — or God, to become the messengers, the aiders, the destructions of hindrances; as the ways between man's approach to — as was represented in the ways of dividing man's knowledge of or between — good and evil. Hence they work ever as those influences or forces that stand between, as it were; being the helpful influences that become as the powers of activity in the very nature or force of man.   281-29

Q-7. What is meant by the four beasts?

A-7. As given, the four destructive influences that make the greater desire for the carnal forces, that rise as the beasts within self to destroy. Even as man, in his desire to make for companionship, brought those elements within self's own experience. These must be met. Even as the dragon represents the one that separated self so far as to fight with, to destroy with, those that would make of themselves a kingdom of their own.   281-16

Q-9. Voice from 4 horns before the throne.

A-9. As indicated by the horns of the altar, as indicated by the 4 forces in nature, as indicated by the 4 influences in the experiences of the individual soul which cry then in the voice raised as a sweet incense, or as the essence of the purifying that has come to the individual entity or soul to arise before the Throne of Him who is Lord of Lords and King of Kings, for His love as given, as shown in that as accomplished in the raising of self in the Christ, the Son, in Jesus.   281-31

Q-20. Pituitary — Silence?

A-20. Silence, golden; the forces upon which the greater expression has been set of all the influences of might and power as may be seen in man's experience — *Silence* if ye would hear the Voice of thy Maker!

Q-30. How should the Lord's Prayer be used in this connection?

A-30. As in feeling, as it were, the flow of the meanings of each portion of same throughout the body-physical. For as there is the response to the mental representations of all of these in the *mental* body, it may build into the physical body in the manner as He, thy Lord, thy brother, so well expressed in, "I have bread ye know not of."   281-29

The *wisdom* gained through the purification of the vibrations of each of the seven centers does indeed become golden. As the centers are united in the oneness of the Creative Forces, the combined vibrations become pure white, spilling over from the pituitary and flowing harmoniously throughout the spiritual, mental and physical bodies, giving peace, joy, happiness and beauty unknown in any other experience. It is then that we can truly say, "My cup runneth over."

Chapter Five

INDIGO

In his booklet *Auras* Edgar Cayce wrote: "Indigo and violet indicate seekers of all types, people who are searching for a cause or a religious experience. As these people get settled in their careers and in their beliefs, however, these colors usually settle back into deep blue. It seems that once the purpose is set in the right direction, blue is a natural emanation of the soul. Those who have purple are inclined to be overbearing, for here there is an infiltration of pink. Heart trouble and stomach trouble are rather common to persons with indigo and violet and purple in their auras."

Indigo, a slightly longer wavelength than violet, is associated in the readings with the *pineal* gland, the church *Philadelphia* in the Revelation, the planet *Mercury,* and *Name* in the Lord's Prayer.

The pineal is located just above the third ventricle within the brain. It is somewhat smaller than the pituitary gland and is attached to the mid-brain by the habenular and posterior commissures. Scientific data suggest that the pineal is a vestigial organ, possibly a remnant of a third eye.

The Cayce readings suggest, however, that the pineal is that center wherein the *pattern,* or the seed, is implanted.

In the unopened state, the pineal receives those vibrations or wavelengths we choose to call *indigo.* Indigo is the color of the *ideal* or *perfect* gland which is the computer storage library of all that the soul has ever done. Whatever the person's memory may be, if it is to be recalled, it will be recalled from this memory bank. Whether this universal awareness is expressed as *personality* or as *individuality* is up to each person. If the choice is positive, if the individuality is expressed in the Universal Awareness of the pineal center, the gland can be opened or attuned and move up into the purple or violet range.

Mercury is the planet of indigo, of the pineal center. It rules the mind, reasoning and the intellect. It governs communications, whether written or spoken, and it controls the arms, hands, lungs, tongue, intestines, and the sense of vision. In other words, all of the five senses are under the Mercurian influence. The readings tell us:

> Mercury brings the high mental abilities; the faculties that at times may become the developing for the soul, or at others [be] turned to the aggrandizement of selfish interests.
>
> For the entity is among those who have entered the earth during those years when there was the great entrance of those who have risen high in their abilities, and who are then passing through those periods when there must be the application of the will, else the very abilities that have been maintained in the Sun and Mercurian influences will become as stumbling blocks . . .   633-2

Astrologers maintain that through the Mercurian influence we receive the positive abilities of a logical nature, discernment, enthusiasm and cheerfulness, and the negative abilities of over-cautiousness, impetuosity and argumentativeness. Having this Mercurian influence indicates high intellectual and reasoning faculties, excellent powers of concentration, and a good memory.

If we summarize the traits indicated in the readings, in the Revelation, and in the planetary influences, then, we find that a preference for indigo would be indicative of high mental abilities, a logical, discerning, enthusiastic and cheerful nature, and a desire to express creativeness with little thought of one's own ego. A dislike for indigo would suggest an overcautious, impetuous and argumentative nature, with a desire to give the ego full play, possibly resulting in a depressed mental state if egocentricities are not fulfilled.

Color psychologists have nothing to say about the color indigo. However, since indigo is a combination of violet and blue something can be gained by looking at the meanings color psychologists ascribe to these colors.

An individual with a preference for the blue-violet or violet-blue combination is searching for an idealized harmony into which he can blend. He has a desire for sympathy and love and is responsive to anything that is esthetic and tasteful. He is, in fact, seeking to share a warm intimacy with a sensitive and understanding partner in an esthetic atmosphere of peace and love.

On the other hand, the rejection of the blue-violet or violet-blue combination is an indication that the individual's existing situation is unsatisfactory. His egocentricities cause him to feel isolated and alone while, at the same time, he is unable to allow himself to form any deep attachments. This in turn inhibits his ability to satisfy the need for affectionate give-and-take, leaving him with a tied-down feeling. He becomes impatient, irritable and feels a compulsion to escape.

Very few will prefer this color due to the lack of harmony in their emotions and thoughts. In most cases, this lack of harmony will be reflected in a dislike for the color indigo.

> Few people, few individual souls really enjoy the companionship of themselves. Not merely because they love themselves the less or that they despise themselves the more. But their thoughts and things and the emotions of the body, are seldom in accord one with the other — or their individuality and their personality don't reflect the same shadow in the mirror of life.   3351-1

> The individuality is that builded. The personality is that with which the individual works in its associations with others, and thus finds expression more often in the emotions . . .   2505-1

If the individuality and the personality reflect the same shadow in the mirror we will be well on the way to purity of color, not only in the indigo of the pineal but in the harmony of the full spectrum.

Chapter Six

BLUE

You will rarely find individuals being intolerant with others with something intrinsically carved being worn — or never very, very mad with blue being worn . . .   578-2

"Blue has always been the color of the spirit," Cayce wrote in *Auras,* "the symbol of contemplation, prayer, and heaven. The sky is blue because gas molecules in the air cause light rays from the sun to be scattered . . .

"Almost any kind of blue is good," he says, "but the deeper shades are the best. Pale blue indicates little depth, but a struggle toward maturity. The person may not be talented but he tries. He will have many heartaches and many headaches, but he will keep going in the right direction. The middle blue, or aqua, belongs to a person who will work harder and get more done than the fellow with light blue, though there may be little difference between them in talent. Those with the deep blue have found their work and are immersed in it. They are apt to be moody and are almost always unusual persons, but they have a mission and they steadfastly go about fulfilling it. They are spiritual minded for the most part, and their life is usually dedicated to an unselfish cause, such as science, art, or social service. I have seen many Sisters of Mercy with this dark blue, and many writers and singers also."

The color blue was synonymous with the highest attainments of the soul according to the early Church. The readings associate the color blue with the *thyroid* gland, the church *Sardis,* the planet *Uranus,* and *will* in the Lord's Prayer.

The thyroid is a divided, or two-lobed, endocrine gland located in the throat on either side of the windpipe or trachea. It is connected below the larynx by a thin isthmus of tissue and is very high in iodine content. The thyroid follicle is the functioning unit of the gland. The rate of oxidation in the body (heat production) and of sugar metabolism is increased when the thyroid hormone is secreted into the blood stream. This hormone also promotes the growth and ossification of bones, aids in the development of the teeth, and is a stimulant to the nervous system, the adrenals and the gonads.

The thyroid gland, and therefore the color blue, has long been associated with man's *will.* The Cayce readings confirm this as well as the fact that the gland is associated with physical growth.

> Then there is the third, that is ever of the feeding or building nature — or the basic cord through which during the period of gestation there is fed the imaginations, as well as the latent response of the body to those conditions external — or that center from which there is drawn the growth in the physical. **281-51**

It is through this center that man's endowment of free will makes itself manifest throughout the physical, mental and spiritual bodies. What we do with this choice determines whether we go forward on the path toward our Maker or whether we further separate ourselves from the Creative Forces

> That man has been endowed with free will, free choice, is his birthright. Do not cast it aside, nor sell it for the gratifying of any material thing in thy experience that is merely passing . . .
> The *choice* must be within thine *own* self.
> The ways may be set before thee — the *choices* must be *taken* of thine own consciousness. Being aware of what ye would that the Lord would do with thee, what *thou* would do with the opportunities, the privileges He hath bestowed upon thee as one of His children. **1470-2**

Whichever choice one makes for himself will be manifested in the ideal he has set. If that ideal is material, the choice will be manifested in materiality. If the ideal is set in the Christ-Consciousness, the choice will manifest itself in the spiritual.

Just how is this choice reflected in the association of the color blue? If the use of the will is for selfish purposes, if the ideal is set strictly in the self's personality and the development of personality for self-aggrandizement, there will probably be a lack of blue in the individual's color scheme. A misuse of will, even though it may result in the achievement of the goals the individual has set for himself, can result in a condition known as hyper-thyroidism. The individual will have to meet every condition the hard way, and very likely he will be nervous and excitable in the process.

On the other hand, if one chooses to make his will one with the Creative Forces, he will have a preference for purity in blue, and will find his way made easier, his load lighter. A preference for blue, particularly those shades with purity and clarity, indicates a spiritual quality, a calm, even, likeable disposition. An individual with such a preference will express himself with thoughtfulness towards others.

"Blue is a color of universal appeal," according to Birren. He writes: "In practically all tests of preference it holds top place . . . an appreciation of blue increases in almost direct proportion to higher education, greater refinement, and higher income.

"Blue is the color of deliberation and introspection, conservatism, and an acceptance of obligations. While those who favor it probably have reflective minds and honest intentions, they sometimes use reason to selfish and self-justified ends."

A genuine love for blue, he says, indicates a sensitiveness to others and to yourself, as well as a firm hold on passions and enthusiasms. Beliefs and opinions of "blue-types" are usually inflexible and firmly set. On the negative side, ideas and ideals of others are sometimes viewed impatiently.

A calm and smoothly-operating environment, with no disturbing upsets, is the goal of one who favors blue, according to Dr. Luscher. Such a person is looking for quiet personal relationships with no frictions whatever.

It has been suggested that Uranus, the planet associated with the color blue, is the planet of *change*. Astrologers indicate that those who have Uranus in their charts express creativity, originality and individuality, and that this planet influences the direction they take in trying to express this individuality. Uranus is also concerned with occultism, originality, altruism and independence.

> Each planetary influence vibrates at a different rate of vibration. An entity entering that influence enters that vibration: [it is] not necessary that he change, but it is the grace of God that he may! It is part of the universal consciousness, the universal law.   281-55

If we consider these aspects in relation to the color blue perhaps an individual who does not have pure blue in his list of color preferences can change his personality, and by trying to develop a taste for pure blue may help to bring his self-will into line with the will of the Creative Forces.

Chapter Seven

GREEN

"Pure emerald green, particularly if it has a dash of blue, is the color of healing. It is helpful, strong, friendly." So states the booklet, *Auras.* "It is the color of doctors and nurses, who invariably have a lot of it in their auras. However, it is seldom a dominating color, usually being over-shadowed by one of its neighbors. As it tends toward blue it is more helpful and trustworthy. As it tends toward yellow it is weakened. A lemony green, with a lot of yellow, is deceitful. As a rule the deep, healing green is seen in small amounts, but it is good to have a little of it in your aura."

Green is the color of grass, plants, and leaves in the spring and summer of life. It is life vibrating in growth.

> . . . colors influence the entity a great deal more even than musical forces in its tone – or color in music. Drabs, or certain greens, have an effect that is almost that to bring *illness* in the physical body; while the purples or violets, or shades of tan, bring an exultant influence that would make for the bringing of building influences in the entity. 428-4

The readings further associate the color green with the *thymus* gland, the church *Thyatira,* the planet *Venus,* and *evil* in the Lord's Prayer. It symbolized youthfulness and fertility in the early Church.

Medical books generally classify the thymus as a ductless gland of uncertain function in the vertebrate animals. It is a fairly large gland situated in the thorax near the base of the neck. It decreases in size after puberty. The lymphoid cortex becomes thin in adults and the epithelial cells of the medulla become compressed, finally being replaced by fat. The word *thymus* is derived from the Greek *thymos,* which means sweetbread. Some scientists believe that this gland secretes a hormone which hastens sexual maturity.

The readings infer that the thymus is the heart center, and some students consider it the seat of the self-conscious mind. As long as the thymus gland is kept active in love and faith, there will be an abundance of white blood cells, the epithelial cells, that guard the body and keep it free from disease. If we neglect and forget the commandment to love others as we love ourselves, this gland will fall from use, or it will become vestigial. According to the readings, selfishness is the only sin. It behooves each of us to make the positive choice to love others so that this gland can be reactivated to immunize the physical, mental and spiritual bodies against all disease.

Green is a passive and self-regulating color, according to color psychologists, and it has an astringent sensation physiologically. It is cool, fresh, and soothing in its appealing beauty. It has the universal appeal of nature in its sense of balance and normality.

Birren says that if you love green "you probably dwell in the great forest of humanity: you are a respectable neighbor, homebuilder, parent, voter, patronizer, joiner." He indicates further that green suggests a retreat from anxieties.

The green personality, according to Luscher, is trying to overpower opposition in order to attain recognition. Such a person is determined enough to exert his will toward his own ends and independence.

Venus, the planet the readings associate with the color green, is generally referred to by astrologers as the *love* planet. It offers such positive gifts as joyfulness, attraction, sweetness, gentleness and harmony. It stimulates the beautification of one's surroundings and acts as a peacemaker. How like nature! What can be more peaceful and beautiful than a walk through a lush, green forest on a summer day?

> In the astrological aspects we find that, through influences from sojourns in the Venus environs, the entity is a lover of beauty; especially of song.
>
> And there should be given training and development, and the awakening for the entity in those influences pertaining to a knowledge of, and the channel for the expression of, the abilities for the use of the entity's voice in *praise* and in thanksgiving . . .
>
> Hence all things that have to do with phases of man's ability of expression in beautiful ways and manners will be of interest to the entity — whether pertaining to nature, to voice or song, or even to art subjects.
>
> 1990-3
>
> In Venus the body-form is near to that [which is] in the three-dimensional plane. For it is what may be said to be rather *all*-inclusive! For it

is that ye would call love — which, to be sure, may be licentious, selfish; which also may be so large, so inclusive as to take on the less of self and more of the ideal, more of that which is *giving*.   5755-1

According to the chapter on love in *A Search for God,* Book I, "There is love manifested in the performance of duty when there is no thought of personal gain, in speaking encouraging words to those seeking an understanding, and in the activities of those doing their best with the talents entrusted to them."

Growth comes from love. Forgiveness comes from love. Opportunities come from love.

   . . . much will come to thee in the knowledge of the fact that law, love, are one — even as the forces in all nature are one . . .   900-428

Chapter Eight

YELLOW

In the readings the vibratory wavelength we call *yellow* is associated with the *adrenal* glands, the church *Pergamos,* the planet *Mars,* and *debts* in the Lord's Prayer.

Edgar Cayce, in *Auras,* wrote: "When it is golden yellow it indicates health and well-being. Such people take good care of themselves, don't worry, and learn easily; good mentality is natural to them. They are happy, friendly, and helpful. If the yellow is ruddy, they are timid. If they are red-heads they are apt to have an inferiority complex. They are thus apt often to be indecisive and weak in will, inclined to let others lead them."

It is interesting to note that the outer three-fourths of the adrenal gland, that part forming the cortex or rind, is deep yellow in color. The medulla, or central core, is dark red. It is also interesting to note that the Cayce readings tell us that the adrenal gland, or solar plexus, is yellow in its normal state but becomes red when opened in meditation.

Situated in front of and slightly above the upper pole of each kidney, the two adrenal, or suprarenal, glands are small, flat, cup-shaped bodies. The cortex, quite essential to life, secretes hormones which play indispensable regulatory roles. Of these, the sugar hormones regulate metabolism, particularly the burning of glucose (sugar). The salt hormones, on the other hand, maintain the mineral balance, mainly between sodium and potassium, and govern the content of water in the body. Adrenalin and noradrenalin are two hormones secreted by the medulla, or central core, of the adrenal glands. It is through these hormones that the rate and power of the heartbeat is stepped up and blood vessels are constricted to raise the blood pressure.

Both the cortex and the medulla perform interrelated functions which cause the body to react to the stress of injury, infection, temperature extremes, or psychic strain. The defenses against infection are lowered when the body is fatigued.

Thus, it is evident that this is the center wherein our fears are emphasized, where our guilt complexes are made known. Dirty yellow in this area reflects cowardice while bright yellow indicates a willingness to call upon the inner being to display the "red badge of courage."

The readings refer to this center as the gland of the solar plexus:

> Then there becomes the first indication of individuality being established in that movement which has come about in its growth, its evolvement; or the gland of the solar plexus, or that *ye* misinterpret and call the adrenals — as they act with the emotions and the growth and unfoldment of the body itself. 281-51

The misuse of the energies received through the yellow wavelength can result in the loss of unregenerate cells through emotional upsets — ulcers, metabolism and mineral imbalance, fears and lack of purpose. The positive use of bright yellow can lead to the regeneration of cells and perfect emotional harmony.

Medical science has determined that three groups of sex hormones are found in the cortex of the adrenal glands and that these seem to bear the same function as the sex hormones secreted by the Cells of Leydig. In reading 281-53 there is the indication that the life force moves from the lyden center to the solar plexus in the growth process. The following statement was given to Cayce to be verified in a reading: "The life force crosses the solar plexus each time it passes to another center."

> In growth, yes. In meditation, yes and no; if there remains the balance as of the attunement, yes . . .
> You see, what takes place in the developing body, or in life growth (which we have used as the demonstration, or have illustrated), may be different from that which takes place as one attempts to meditate and to distribute the life force in order to aid another — or to control the influence as in healing, or to attain to an attunement in self for a deeper or better understanding. These questions or statements are such that they will be confusing to some; but if they are asked properly there will not be confusion. 281-53

If Mars, as the astrologers say, is the planet of energy or sex, we might speculate that *yellow* is the color of energy or sex, for the readings tell us that Mars is the planet associated with the solar plexus. Consequently we can assign to yellow the positive traits of creativeness, inventiveness, constructivity, endless energy, forcefulness, powerfulness, courage, self-confidence and strength of character, as well as the negative traits of strife, pugnacity, self-assertiveness and anger.

Although Mars is generally referred to as the "red" planet, it is interesting to note that physically its associated gland is both yellow and red and that the combination of these two colors, orange, is the color associated with the lyden center. No wonder, then, that Mars is referred to as the planet of energy, sex, creativity or even of frustration.

Could it be that a decided preference for yellow would indicate that a person has learned his lessons from a sojourn in the influence of Mars, and has overcome the selfish urges of anger and aggression? Or is this mastery only achieved when the entity goes deeper inward to the red of the adrenals' core in the meditative process?

> For the inclinations from the Martian influences are for anger to easily arise in the experiences when the entity is fraught in its activities, in the associations, in its determinations.
>
> And it usually has its way, unless there is reason and love and care and precaution shown by those that direct the developing or formative periods.   1434-1

Another reading tells us that even though these urges may become a part of the physical experience, it is really the will that determines what the individual soul will do with his opportunities. Blue, the color of the will, blends well with yellow. Together they form green, the color of healing. An impure blue combined with an impure yellow results in a drab green, a color that can bring illness in the physical body. ("Drabs, or certain greens, have an effect that is almost that to bring *illness* in the physical body . . . " 428-4)

Sunlight, cheerfulness and happiness are associated with yellow. Yellow acts in much the same manner as red in increasing blood pressure, pulse and respiration rates.

"Prefer yellow and your thoughts are certain to be neatly formed," writes Faber Birren. "You are very much impressed by your intellectual capacity. Your dreams, if any, are inclined to be lofty. You are anxious to help the world and all people in terms of what the world and people seem to need in your eyes. You have a special love for things that are contemporary and challenging."

He goes on to say that a person who prefers yellow is inclined to be aloof from others, that he has the greatest of intentions but seldom does anything about them. This type of person, though shy, probably controls his temper well but is more inclined to put up with people rather than express a feeling of love for them.

Mr. Birren also says that "To reject yellow is to reject newness and innovation. If you are so inclined, it is likely that you also reject the fanciful, the imaginative, the occult, and everything that touches the abstract. You prefer to concentrate on reality, on the particulars at hand."

Chapter Nine

ORANGE

"Orange is the color of the sun. It is vital, and a good color generally, indicating thoughtfulness and consideration of others. Again, however, it is a matter of shade. Golden orange is vital and indicates self-control, whereas brownish orange shows a lack of ambition and a don't care attitude. Such people may be repressed, but usually they are just lazy. People with orange in their auras are subject to kidney trouble." *(Auras)*

It must be remembered that these observations on color were made in the *waking* state and refer to Edgar Cayce's ability to see the aura surrounding individuals. Although there is a relationship between these vibrations and the color vibrations associated with the individual glands, the interpretations are not always correlative.

The psychic readings given by Cayce, particularly those referred to as the Revelation readings, indicate an association between the *orange* vibrations and the *lyden* center, or Cells of Leydig, the church *Smyrna,* the planet *Neptune,* and *temptation* in the Lord's Prayer. Orange was symbolic of glory, virtue and the fruits of the earth in the early Church. All of these symbols are naturally related to the sun, the principal source of our light.

During reading 281-53 Hugh Lynn Cayce made the statement that "the Leydig gland is the same as that we have called the lyden, and is located in the gonads." The answer given was:

> It is in and above, or the activity passes through the gonads. Lyden is the meaning — or the seal, see? while Leydig is the name of the individual who indicated this was the activity. You can call it either of these that you want to.   281-53

Writers of medical books on human anatomy, in describing the gonads (testes in the male and ovaries in the female), tell us that there are coils of seminiferous tubules in the testes in which the spermatozoa are formed. Nests of cells, the interstitial Cells of Leydig, are found in the connective tissue between these seminiferous tubules. It is thought that these interstitial cells secrete the male sex hormone, testosterone. The female sex hormone known as progesterone produces secretory changes in the uterine endometrium and inhibits uterine contractility.

The lyden center, or these interstitial cells, is the "seat of the soul" according to reading 3969-1. Another reading indicates that it is through the Leydig center that the soul expresses itself in its creative nature. In other words, it is the combination of the creativeness of red (gonads) and yellow (adrenals) that produces orange (lyden).

> Then in the physical body there *are* those influences, then, through which each of these phases of an entity may or does become an active influence.
>
> There may be brought about an awareness of this by the exercising of the mind, through the manner of directing the breathing.
>
> For, in the body there is that center in which the soul is expressive, creative in nature – the Leydig center.
>
> By this breathing, this may be made to expand – as it moves along the path that is taken in its first inception, at conception, and opens the seven centers of the body that radiate or are active upon the organisms of the body.
>
> This in its direction may be held or made to be a helpful influence for specific conditions, at times – by those who have taught, or who through experience have found as it were the key, or that which one may do and yet must not do; owing to whatever preparation has been made or may be made by the body for the use of this ability, this expression through the body-forces.
>
> As this life-force is expanded, it moves first from the Leydig center through the adrenals, in what may be termed an upward trend, to the pineal and to the centers in control of the emotions – or reflexes through the nerve forces of the body.   2475-1

In describing this life force, with which the orange vibration is associated, the following reading states that there are two life forces.

> One life force is the body-growth, as just described. The other is the impulse that arises, from the life center, in meditation.   281-53

In the same reading:

> *Q-4. The life force crosses the solar plexus each time it passes to another center.*
>
> A-4. In growth, yes. In meditation, yes and no; if there remains the balance as of the attunement, yes.

It would seem, then, that orange is indicative of creative expression, the spark of genius. Because it is associated with two of the four lower centers, or *earth,* it would be expressive of earthiness and nature.

In the physical sense, this nest of interstitial cells, referred to in the readings as the lyden center, is an integral part of the gonad glands. The readings suggest that the initial creative energy is activated by the gonads, moves upward to the pituitary by way of the adrenals and back again to the lyden center where the purposes and ideals are formulated.

The lyden center, and consequently orange, is also related in the readings to the planet Neptune. The astrological readings should give us further insight into the personality of the *orange* type.

> In Neptune, [we find] those of the mysticism, mystery, spiritual insight, spiritual development. 900-14

> From Neptune we find . . . those abilities as the mystic — the interest in the unusual, as in the abilities of seeing, feeling, experiencing that which to most would be the unseen forces about the entity. 2308-1

> . . . we have an entity that to self and all others . . . will be peculiar to other people, rarely ever being understood; yet one with the spiritual insight of the developing in the earth plane, and one whom others would be, could be, benefited by, by being in contact with this entity. 2553-1

The artistic temperament is derived from sojourns in the influence of Neptune, apparently, and is reflected in a preference for orange.

> In Neptune, the artistic temperament — both as to material things and the mental or spiritual relationships. Remember the beautiful ever, and look for the agreements rather than for disagreements. Do not condemn that which has not been applied nor that self has not experienced in the same character of circumstance. Thus, never repeat that which might be harmful to anyone, even though it be only gossip for the moment.
> 1533-2

Orange and blue used together may be considered a bit unusual by some people, but it is an interesting combination.

> Neptune *and* Uranus make for an interest in reading matter that is of an unusual nature. Things that pertain to mysteries, or conditions in individuals' or groups' lives that are unusual, the uncanny and such . . .
> 406-1

Imagine, if you will, a color combination of orange, blue, green and red: the expression of the Creative Forces, plus the will, plus love, plus the life force itself. If each of these are pure in color, an individual with these influences would be a most unusual person, a person who would be influential with others. Negative, or impure colors, would suggest an unusually weird personality. Such a combination was indicated in the following reading.

> In the astrological aspects we find Neptune, Uranus, Venus and Saturn as the greater influence . . . Hence we will find the inclination for seeking the unusual places, strange conditions — taking up with and associating with strange surroundings, having strange playmates — the desire for unusual in pets . . .   2005-1

Another reading suggests that an individual with a combination of violet, green and orange is a person of learning, but one who uses his learning to exalt himself.

> . . . we find those inclinations: With the strength of Jupiter forces, with that of Venus and Neptune, we find one given to letters, and of high exalted positions of self and all concerned therewith. Given to make show, or display, of that element that gives the greater expression of self. Hence, will must be directed, else with the influence of Venus' forces would give detrimental elements in the life.   4228-1

If orange is a favored color, according to Birren, one is "social by nature, able to get along with all types of human beings — saints and sinners, wrestlers, intellectuals, rich and poor." Such an individual has a sincere desire to "like people and to be liked in return," but there may be fickleness in friendships.

Luscher says the individual with an orange preference wants to be successful in whatever he does. He is looking for stimulation and is seeking the experiencing of life to its fullest. Such an individual wants to win constantly and live life intensely with no self-doubts. He is a freedom-loving spirit who enjoys contacts with others, is naturally enthusiastic and is receptive to all that is new or intriguing. This individual is optimistic about his future, constantly seeking to expand his activities and many interests.

Chapter Ten

RED

The longest wavelength in the visible spectrum is red. It is an outgoing vibration related to aggressiveness and conquest. It is an expression of vitality, of nervousness and glandular activity. It is an exciting color.

Red vibrations stimulate the autonomic nervous system by speeding up the rate of the heartbeat and the rise and fall of the respiratory organs, and by increasing the blood pressure. The autonomic nervous system through which this is effected is a self-regulating system that operates below the threshold of awareness.

If red is seen in one's aura, according to Edgar Cayce, "it indicates force, vigor and energy." The relationship to other colors, as well as the shade of red, must be considered in determining the meaning of the color, he suggested. "Dark red indicates high temper," he wrote, "and it is a symbol of nervous turmoil. A person with dark red in his aura may not be weak outwardly, but he is suffering in some way, and it is reflected in his nervous system. Such a person is apt to be domineering and quick to act. If the shade of red is light, it indicates a nervous, impulsive, very active person, one who is probably self-centered. Scarlet indicates an overdose of ego. Pink, or coral, is the color of immaturity. It is seen usually in young people, and if it shows up in the aura of one who is grown it indicates delayed adolescence, a childish concern with self. In all cases of red there is a tendency to nervous troubles, and such people ought to take time to be quiet and to get outside of themselves." *(Auras)*

The *gonad,* according to the Cayce readings, is the endocrine gland associated with the color red, as is the church *Ephesus,* the planet *Saturn,* and *bread* in the Lord's Prayer.

This gland, the testes in the male and the ovaries in the female, is a *paired* gland which, in association with accessory reproductive glands, is the center that activates the life force in the creative process.

Is the First Cause, then, that the separation of God in the desire for companionship with Himself, that as created or brought into a material manifestation the reverse of love, of hope, of patience, of all the attributes that are the spirit of activity, the moving influence or force?

This we see manifested in a physical body through the glandular system — as the activity of conception, the dividing of the activity of the gland itself, that brings conception.   281-51

This urge for beginning or activating creativity is also set forth in the readings on astrology, on the planet Saturn:

From Saturn we find the tendency for the starting of new experiences, the starting of new associations in the activities; and unless these are tempered with the mental influences they are rarely carried to their full termination. This again would be as a warning . . . When thou hast chosen that direction, that activity thou would take, know that thou art kept in a balance that is of the material, mental and spiritual influences near to right. Then lay it not aside until it, the activity, has borne fruit in thine mental and material experience.   361-4

Astrologists differ from the Cayce readings somewhat when they suggest that the Saturnian influence brings about a high degree of organization, scientific interests, reclusiveness, solid convictions with depth of character, dependability, prudent, sober good sense and patience. The readings suggest rather that the activating urge is toward a testing period.

In Saturn we find the sudden or violent changes — those influences and environs that do not grow, as it were, but are sudden by that of change of circumstance, materially, or by activities apparently [on] the part of others that become a part of self in the very associations. And these are testing periods of thy endurance, of thy patience, of thy love of truth, harmony and the spirit that faileth not.

From the combination of this with Uranus we find the extremes; the environs materially or mentally in which the very opposites may be expected. Remember, only in Christ, Jesus, do extremes meet.   1981-1

The readings also suggest that the influence of Saturn, and thus of the red vibration, brings with it a muddling or instability in activities.

In Saturn we find the inclinations for changes, as to this, that or the other; and to muddle a great many things together in the activity.

Hence that injunction as given by the sages of old, "The merchant is never the student; neither is the student ever the merchant," should be as a part of the entity's program in its choice of its activity in this experience.
                                          1426-1

Seemingly, when one has misused too many of God's laws in an earthly existence the soul must seek a sojourn in the influence of Saturn, or red, to work out his need for change.

> Those then of the experience must be tempered rather with the activities that come from environmental as well as the expressions of the Venus influence.
>
> While the Venus influences are latent, these should find the greater expression; else the urges as from Saturn would make for the entity having *many* homes, or many marriages — and these are *not* well in the experience if there are to be the developments.
>
> For consistency and persistency are the sister of patience; patience the entity needs to learn as its lesson in this experience.   1431-1

Red, orange and blue influence the desire to travel and to make changes, as well as stimulate interest in, and the fear of, the mystical and the occult.

> In the astrological activities that produce or bring about these experiences [the desire for travel, desire for change of scene and environ] as innate, we find Uranus, Neptune and Saturn as ruling influences; which make for the interest in yet the fear of occult and mystic forces. But rather if there is the activity and the expression of the psychic, rather than the occult *or* mystic, we may find greater development, greater experiences for the entity.   1431-1

The red vibration is the spirit of activity, a moving influence. A preference for that color denotes a strong sex drive, a creativeness, a desire for new things and new friends, for travel and change, both in environment and friends. Its negative aspect is an aggressive, war-like attitude, self-centeredness and instability. It may suggest an interest in the mystical and the occult.

According to Birren, there is an outward direction to your life if you favor red. The positiveness of red vibrations carries with it aggressiveness, vigor, impulsiveness in emotion and activity. There is a tendency toward abruptness and earthiness in the manner of one who favors red, as well as impatience. There is a fickleness in feelings and sympathies for other people and there is a strong sex drive. "To those who like red, however, life is meant to be happy," he writes, "and they are upset when it isn't."

Red accelerates the rate of the pulse and of respiration and raises the blood pressure. It denotes a vibrant force. It is an indication of nervous and glandular stimulation. A preference for red clearly mirrors desire or fantasy in the relishing of food, sexual potency, achievement of success or the completeness of living. Red personalities want their experiences to be complete and full.

Red, an activating vibration, is a color closely associated with creation itself. It can reflect either constructive creativity or destructive creativity, depending upon the choice made and the purpose for which the activity is set in motion.

Know that choice is made by the will, guided by the mental according to that which — in the consciousness of self — is an entity's ideal. 1885-2

As has been indicated, these are channels, these are opportunities. For what purpose? For fame or fortune alone? or that ye may be a helpful influence? If the motives are selfish, little success. If they are for the universal forces or sources, that God may be the greater glory in the lives of others through thine own feeble effort, then success. For know, ye alone with the Lord are a *great* majority! 1494-1

Chapter Eleven

USE OF COLOR IN DAILY LIFE

Many theories have been expounded on the subject of color and its use in healing, in personality identification, and in the effective use of color harmony in our wearing apparel and surroundings. As has already been stated, we cannot live without color. It is the essence of the life force all about us. Take away the motion of light or color and we would have no awareness at all of the appearance of matter. All knowledge exists in this universal mind-force of Light – this extension of God – if we become one with Him.

> . . . the body mentally – and the body in its nerve reaction – would respond as quickly to color forces as it would to medicinal properties . . .
>
> 4501-1

The use of color, of course, is not the only way to bring about healing. It is only one of many tools with which we are provided, if only we will recognize it and apply it in the proper manner.

> That the manner of healing would be always with color or tone would not be in keeping with the diversity of disturbing influences in others. That this be made the only means may limit the ability, as well as the scope of work that might be accomplished. But begin in the study in association with those influences, if directed there, and be guided in the use of vibration – which is another phase of color, of course, and of tone . . . For, as has so oft been given, and as demonstrated in the experience of the Great Physician, He met the needs of the individual – whether by the spoken word, vibration, or application of means that attune – the dissenting tissue or body to the divinity that is in each soul . . .   2441-4

The average person shuns light and light sources that are decidedly different from daylight or sunlight, but color psychologists are uncertain as to the origin of this objection. It could be psychological or it could be based on some physiological effect as yet undiscovered. At any rate, because of this objection, any illumination should be as natural as possible.

There is something within each of us that makes us respond to this energy which is the essence of the Creative Forces. That is the way the material body is constructed. Each atom within the physical body is emitting wavelengths of color and tone constantly. These wavelengths of energy, or color, are in such combinations within each endocrine gland as to set up individual, or unique, vibrations for each. Each of these spiritual centers, however, must vibrate harmoniously with each other if there is to be harmony and health within the total physical, mental and spiritual body. If the vibration at any one center is out of harmony with itself it would be safe to assume that disease or disharmony exists. Consequently, each of the other of the seven glands would have to work harder to compensate for the inharmonious gland, thereby increasing the possibility of the disruption of total body forces.

To compensate for such possibilities, the Creative Forces give us a continuous source of energy through light. We may think that light and color are given to us purely for beauty but that is not the case. Rather these vibrations are beautiful to us because something within tells us that we need this light in order to be in harmony with ourselves and with others, and so that we may grow and evolve into that which we must.

The pituitary gland transforms the colors of the light rays into revitalizing energies to rebuild those centers that are lacking in energy and to reinforce the energies being created within each gland. For example, an individual whose adrenal gland is disturbed or out of balance will subconsciously reach out for yellow or red. This will be evident in the individual's current color preference, even though the preferred color might be manifested in an impure shade.

To aid in the healing process, the individual should surround himself with pure yellows and reds, whether these colors are pale or strong, in order to supply reinforcing vibrations to the adrenal glands. If the individual applies himself physically, mentally and spiritually through the meditative process to the Creative Forces, healing will be possible.

We must develop a constant awareness that conditions, thoughts and activities are things and that their vibrations, whether color or sound, are felt by others. These vibrations do have an effect upon other entities and things about us.

The color we see in a painting, in the garments we wear or in the rooms we decorate, is not the reality. The reality is in the thought behind the color. Color is only the symbol which conveys the thought, and it has meaning only in the mind of the beholder who finally interprets it. The thought behind the color is never created — it belongs to the thinker and to those who are capable of interpreting the color symbol in which the thought is expressed. It follows, then, that when we are conveying our thoughts to others through the colors we use, we should make certain that our thoughts are pure.

Until we are thoroughly aware that the energy of the thought is the *cause* behind all things and that what we produce is only the *effect*, we are limited in our actions and are enmeshed in the effect. In this limited awareness we are but imitators in an imitative world. We copy but we do not create. However, when we know the principles of light and color and live by them, we will set our knowledge into motion creatively and express ourselves dynamically.

If we realize that the only *things* we ever create are thought forms, and if those forms are true to the balance and rhythm of inspired thought, we will inspire others with that truth. We will know before we begin to create, if we think this way, that our creation will be masterly.

To be creative we must think about our color schemes in order to put meaning into whatever we do with color. We need to apply our own creative forces in those channels which will give light, life and abundance. If we use the harmony of color, its beauty, in the expression of the soul-self, the spirit may flow through and bring healing influences and helpful forces to others.

Color combinations in clothing may have a greater effect upon others than upon ourselves. In putting together a color combination in wearing apparel, we should consider the emotional impact it will have on those with whom we come in contact. Will it antagonize them? Will it drive them away? Or will it pacify and inspire them? A dominant red will stir things up and may even cause anger; it certainly creates the feeling of energy. Too much bold blue may tell the world that we impose *our* wills. Softer shades of blue pacify and calm troubled minds. Adding a little green can produce healing effects.

Selecting colors for the home follows the same basic pattern, though here larger masses of color are used. In this case, we are creating an atmosphere for ourselves and our families as well as for those we invite into our homes. Yellow may stimulate thought, a touch of orange brings warmth, pale blues cool and calm. We should use our imaginations and follow our intuitions to create the color harmonies we want.

The Cayce readings tell us to use our mental self first, then take it to the *deeper within* through meditation.

> In seeking the answer then to any problem, the entity may find same if it will first — the mental self — make definite efforts to gain the answer through its own mental reasoning; analyzing the whole situations much in the same manner as there is a visualizing even before there is a drawing of how an individual room or suite or several would look under the varying treatments with the varying characters of lights or the like, as well as woods and shapes and forms and the like.
>
> If the whole situations are taken into consideration, there must necessarily be first the analysis of the character as it were of the individual for whom such might be prepared.
>
> So, in the analyzing of the problems for self, analyze same much in the same manner; taking into consideration the individuals, their characters, their associations, their background, their outlook upon their relationships with others. And have the answer, Yes or No.
>
> Then take the same considerations, with the answer, into the deep meditation and let there still be the answer from the deeper within — but abide by that given thee! Do not become one that asks and does not abide by the answers! For they would soon become as naught to thee!   1246-4

We have discussed the individual colors in the previous chapters and have already determined that with each of the seven colors, as with everything else, we have a choice: we can use each color vibration constructively or we can use it destructively. We can use it in harmony with the Creative Force or we can use it for selfish or self-satisfying purposes. Awareness of this principle can bring us greater abilities and greater harmonies.

> These awarenesses bring greater abilities, greater harmonies into the experience. Hence they are the beauties — yea, the expressions of that rule and force and manner which should conduct the dealings of one entity with another, in those journeys along that way leading home!
>
> Let that light, that harmony, that peace, take its time with thee. This brings the entity again to that second premise — as it, too, is a part of those awarenesses about the entity, of that love which makes itself manifest. For, if ye would have friends, ye must indeed show thyself friendly. If ye would know God and those relationships to Him, then, ye must seek after Him. For it is the answering of that spirit within thee to that spirit from which it comes.
>
> Thus love thy neighbor as thyself. *Seek* to be that channel that causes those ye meet day by day to be better in every way because of coming in contact with thee . . .   2072-4

We can use color to create any atmosphere we desire so long as we begin with the underlying principles of balance fundamental to all the universe, and as long as we retain the awareness that we have the help of the Creative Force. Our part in building the structure is just as necessary as any other. Our constant goals should be *beauty* and *worthiness* — worthiness to live as masterful interpreters of *Light*.

... all truth, all knowledge, all light, is at the hand of *every* individual. The application of its truth in the experience of an entity must be a *personal* application by self. 333-6

BIBLIOGRAPHY

Babbitt, Edwin D., *The Principles of Light and Color,* University Books, Inc., New Hyde Park, N.Y., 1967

Birren, Faber, *Color in Your World,* The Crowell-Collier Publishing Co., New York, N.Y., 1962

Birren, Faber, *Color Psychology and Color Therapy,* University Books, Inc., New Hyde Park, N.Y., 1961

Bragg, Sir William, *The Universe of Light,* Dover Publications, Inc., New York, N.Y., 1940

Cayce, Edgar, *Auras,* A.R.E. Press, Virginia Beach, Virginia, 1945

Clulow, F.W., *Color — Its Principles and Their Applications,* Morgan & Morgan, Inc., Hastings-on-Hudson, N.Y., 1972

Evans, Ralph M., *An Introduction to Color,* John Wiley & Sons, Inc., New York, N.Y., 1948

Gammon, Margaret H., *Astrology and the Edgar Cayce Readings,* A.R.E. Press, Virginia Beach, Virginia, 1967

Heline, Corinne, *Color and Music in the New Age,* New Age Press, Inc., Oceanside, California, 1964

Heline, Corinne, *Healing and Regeneration Through Color,* J.F. Rowny Press, Santa Barbara, California, 1944

Hessey, J. Dodson, *Colour in the Treatment of Disease,* Rider & Co., London, England

Hunt, Roland T., *Color: Key to the Nu-Clear Age,* CSA Press, Lakemont, Georgia, 1968

Judd, Deane B., *Color Vision — Medical Physics,* Year Book Medical Publishers, Inc., Chicago, 1944

Kandinsky, Wassily, *The Art of Spiritual Harmony,* Houghton Mifflin Company, Boston, 1914

Lancaster-Brown, Peter, *Astronomy in Color,* The Macmillan Company, New York, N.Y., 1972

Luscher, Dr. Max, *The Luscher Color Test,* translated and edited by Ian Scott, Random House, Inc., New York, N.Y., 1943

Mayer, Gladys, *Colour and Healing,* New Knowledge Books, Sussex, England, 1960

Pirenne, M.H., *Vision and the Eye,* Barnes & Noble Books, New York, N.Y., 1967

Podolsky, Edward, M.D., *How to Charm with Color,* Herald Publishing Co., New York, N.Y., 1943

Sechrist, Elsie, *Meditation – Gateway to Light,* A.R.E. Press, Virginia Beach, Virginia, 1964

Winston, Shirley Rabb, *Music as the Bridge,* A.R.E. Press, Virginia Beach, Virginia, 1972

Woodward, Mary Ann, *That Ye May Heal,* A.R.E. Press, Virginia Beach, Virginia, 1970